Crayola World of BLUE

Mari Schuh

Lerner Publications ◆ Minneapolis

For Tabitha, an excellent reader

Official Licensed Product
Lerner Publications Company
A division of Lerner Publishing Group, Inc.
241 First Avenue North
Minneapolis, MN 55401 USA

For reading levels and more information, look up this title at www.lernerbooks.com.

Main body text set in Mikado a Medium 20/28.
Typeface provided by HVD Fonts.

Library of Congress Cataloging-in-Publication Data

The Cataloging-in-Publication Data for *Crayola® World of Blue* is on file at the Library of Congress.
ISBN 978-1-5415-5465-8 (lib. bdg.)
ISBN 978-1-5415-7383-3 (pbk.)
ISBN 978-1-5415-6136-6 (eb pdf)

Manufactured in the United States of America
1-45783-42665-11/5/2018

CONTENTS

Hello, Blue!

Look around. Do you see **blue**?

Navy, **royal blue**, **denim**, and **sky blue** are all shades of **blue**. The world is full of **blue**!

Blue in Nature

You can find **blue** growing in fields and gardens. Bright **blue** petals spread out in the warm summer sun.

Blue is for summer fun.

Want to ride a boat across a big, blue lake?

Look up!

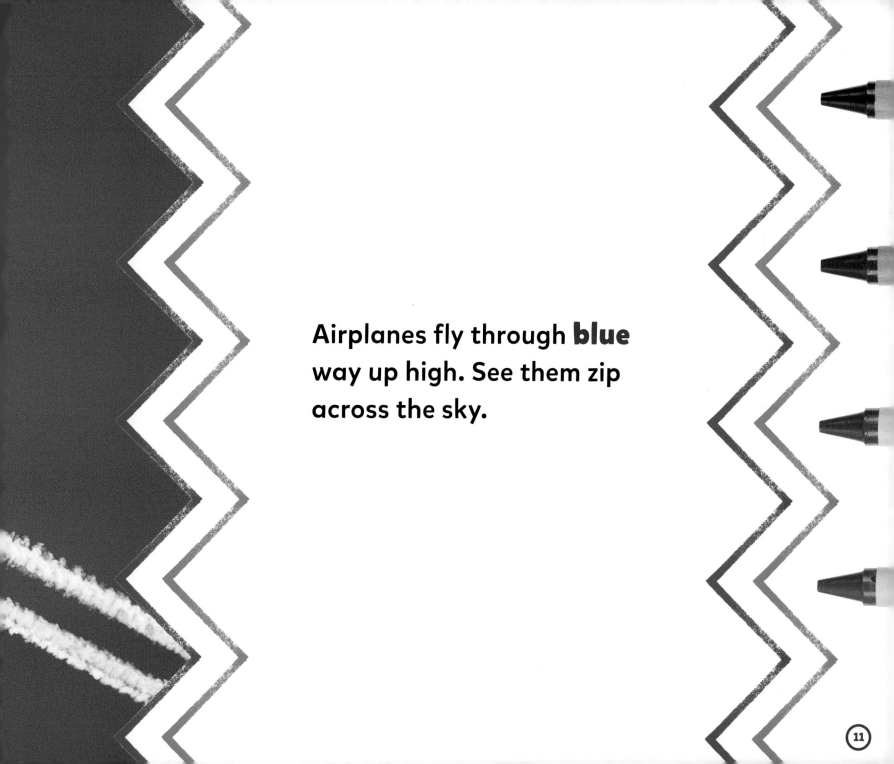

Airplanes fly through **blue** way up high. See them zip across the sky.

Blue Animals

Blue chirps in the trees. Bright feathers keep blue jays and buntings warm and dry.

Blue can be a warning. The rings of this **blue**-ringed octopus warn other animals to stay away!

Colorful **blue** betta fish swim through the dark water.

Blue Foods

Blue is fun to eat.
Plump blueberries
are a tasty treat.
Grab a handful!

Corn on the cob can be a beautiful **blue**.

Yum!

Blue
Where You Live

Blue is at school. It might be on your backpack or in your library. Where can you find **blue** in your classroom?

Blue runs up and down the field. Uniforms bring a team together. Helmets keep players safe.

Go, blue, go!

You can find **blue** close to home. Go for a ride on a **blue** bicycle at the park. Send a birthday card in a blue mailbox.

Where will you find **blue** today?

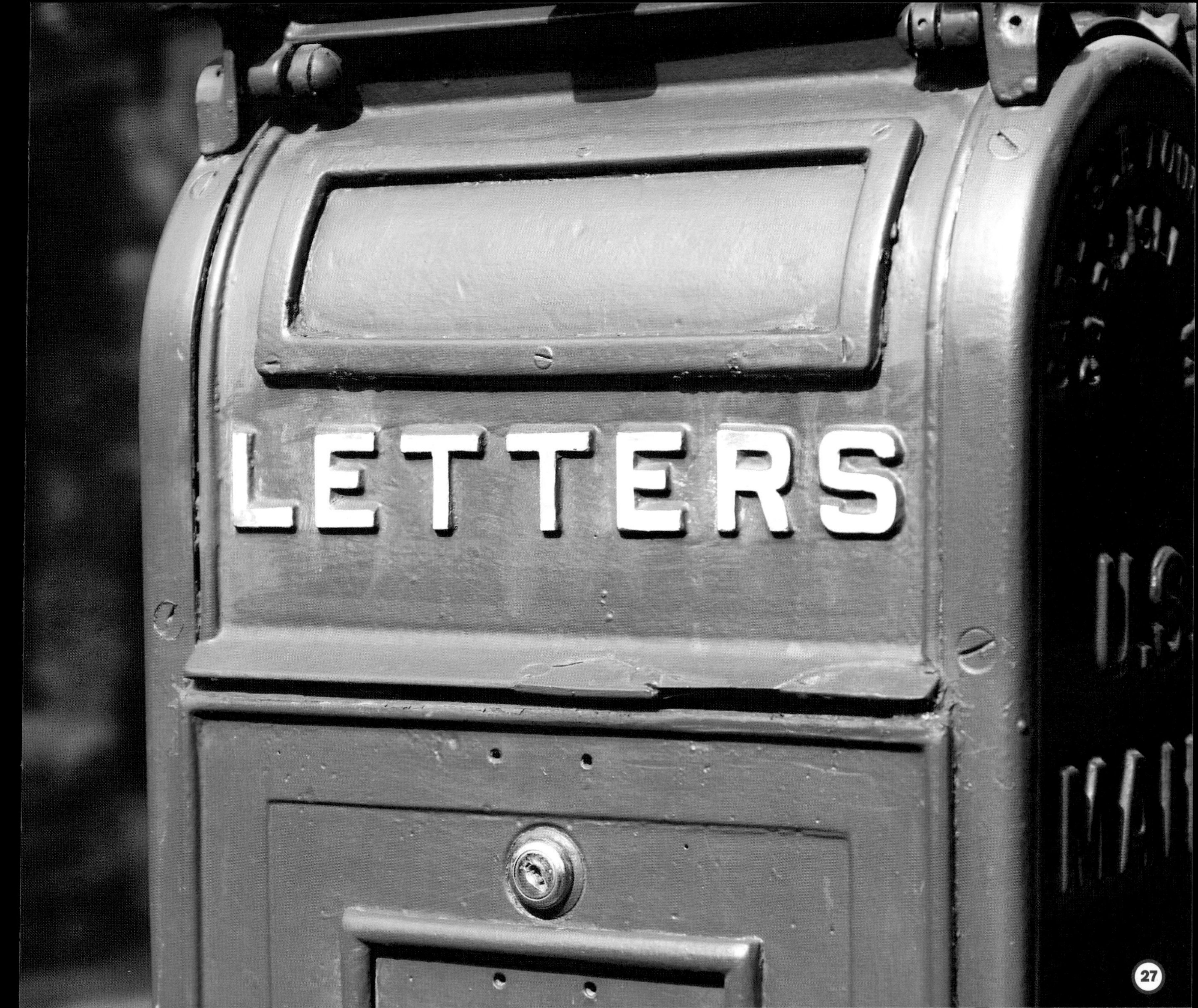
LETTERS

Color with Blue!

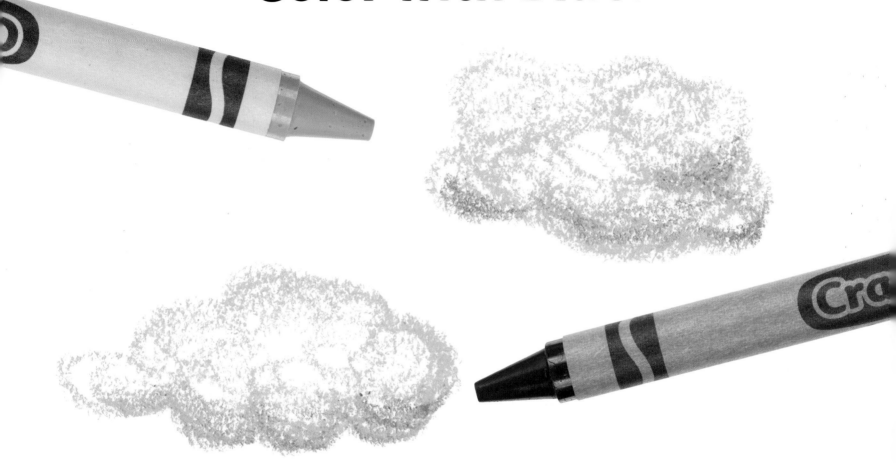

Draw a picture using only **blue** crayons.
What will you draw? How many shades of **blue** will you use?

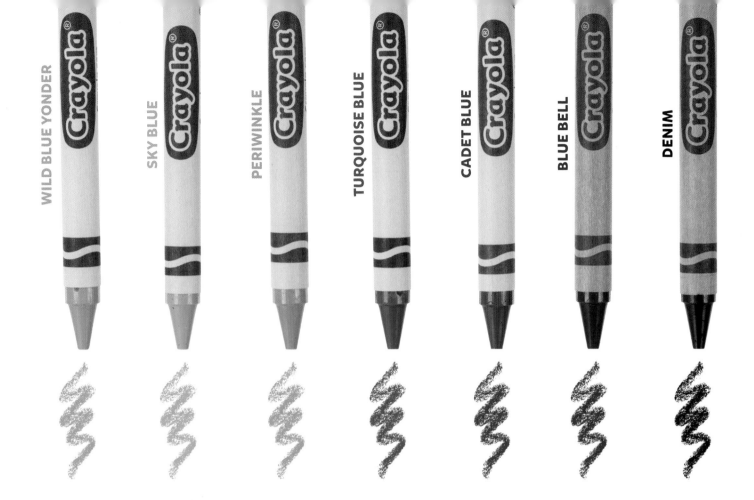

Blue All around Us

Blue is found all around our world. Here are some Crayola® crayon shades of blue used in this book. Can you find them in the photos? Which blue is your favorite?

Glossary

cob: the center part of an ear of corn on which the kernels grow

denim: a strong material used to make jeans and other pieces of clothing

petal: one of the colored outer parts of a flower

poisonous: having a poison that can harm or kill

shade: a color's lightness or darkness

uniform: special clothing worn by sports teams and other groups

warning: telling about a possible danger that might happen

To Learn More

Books

Cantillo, Oscar. *Blue around Me*. New York: Cavendish Square, 2015.
Read this book to find the color blue in things you see every day.

Schuh, Mari. *Crayola Summer Colors*. Minneapolis: Lerner Publications, 2018.
Discover all the colors you can find during summer, including the color blue!

Websites

Crayola Coloring Page: At the Beach
http://www.crayola.com/free-coloring-pages/print/at-the-beach-coloring-page/
Visit this website to color a fun beach scene with beautiful blue waves.

25+ Amazing Blue Animals
https://animalsfacts.net/blue-animals/
How many blue animals are there? Check out this website to find some of your favorites!

Index

Photo Acknowledgments

Image credits: suwatsilp sooksang/Shutterstock.com, p. 2; fullempty/Shutterstock.com, p. 4 (flower); Ruslan Semichev/Shutterstock.com, p. 4 (jeans); Pan Xunbin/Shutterstock.com, pp. 4–5 (lizard); Brocreative/Shutterstock.com, p. 5 (kids); Beth Swanson/Shutterstock.com, p. 5 (wave); PremiumArt/Shutterstock.com, p. 6; Shulevskyy Volodymyr/Shutterstock.com, pp. 6–7; ian woolcock/Shutterstock.com, pp. 8–9; GeoStock/Photodisc/Getty Images, pp. 10–11; FotoRequest/Shutterstock.com, p. 12; John L. Absher/Shutterstock.com, pp. 12–13; JumKit/Shutterstock.com, pp. 14–15; Wataru Utada/Shutterstock.com, pp. 16–17; kuvona/Shutterstock.com, p. 18; stonerobertc/iStock/Getty Images, pp. 18–19; tome213/Shutterstock.com, pp. 20–21; artisteer/iStock/Getty Images, p. 22; qushe/Shutterstock.com, pp. 22–23; Laszlo66/Shutterstock.com, pp. 24–25; Valerie Loiseleux/iStock/Getty Images, p. 25; Gemenacom/Shutterstock.com, p. 26; Usa-Pyon/Shutterstock.com, pp. 26–27; Davdeka/Shutterstock.com, p. 28 (blue clouds); zorina_larisa/Shutterstock.com (design elements throughout).

Cover: LazyPixel/Brunner Sébastien/Moment/Getty Images (frog); Elovich/Shutterstock.com (blueberries); John L. Absher/Shutterstock.com (bird); NASA Goddard Space Flight Center (CC BY 2.0) (blue sky).